T.A. Maxwell

I Am Joe American
And Other Poems

Printed in the United States of America
First Printing, 2013
ISBN 0-989018245

Published by Zen Dog Publishing, U.S.A
.zendogpublishing@live.com

ta.maxwell@live.com
www.amazon.com/author/tamaxwell

For Ginsburg, Bukowski, and Hughes

I Am Joe American
and Other Poems

Poet's Note

This collection of poetry is a work in progress. It will be the only book of poetry that I will ever write, but it will continue to expand and evolve over the years. My style has been heavily influence by the spontaneous prose of the Beat Poets of the fifties and beyond. Every poem was written at that moment in time without much editing, which is how I believe poetry should be written. They deal with politics, love, death, and society. Some of them just deal with my insane ramblings and thoughts. I have also included some lyrics at the end that I have written over the years. Enjoy or don't, I could care less. They are mine; I just decided to share them with the world.

I AM JOE AMERICAN

I am Joe American

Living my eighty year plan

Of

Birth

School

Work

And death

Born and raised

A Christian

Without knowing

What that is

Without choices

Without change

Told to accept

The truth

Without knowing

The truth

Not to question

Just believe

What is a Jew?

What is a Hindu?

What is a Buddhist?

What is an Atheist?

Who is Charles Darwin?

I am Joe American

Sitting in a crowded

Classroom

Zoning out

To the monotone ramblings

Of a so-called

"Teacher"

Preparing me for death

Before I can even live

Preparing me

for boredom

Preparing me

for the monotony of work

In a profession

that is not fulfilling

Decades of schooling

To answer phones

Lift boxes

Punch keys on a machine

That is smarter than me

Why can't I be an artist?

Why can't I be a writer?

Why can't I be a poet?

Why can't I just do nothing?

Because there is no money

In these dreams

The arts

and humanities

Are dead

Now get back to work!

But I don't want to work

I want to live

Death is not for another

Fifty years

If money is the root of all evil

Then work is evil

Your cubicle is hell

And your boss is Satan himself

But you need to work

You need to make money

You need to eat

To have a roof over your head

And clothes on your back

You have to raise a family

Buy a sports utility vehicle

Buy a four bedroom

Two and a half bathroom

House

With a white picket fence

And a three car garage

But what if I don't want a family?

What if I don't want an SUV?

What if I don't want a house?

With a three car whatever

I can eat from the earth

I can live in my car

And what's wrong

With the clothes I'm wearing

This dream

This American dream

Is yours

Not mine

Go preach to the choir

I am not buying

your bullshit

Because that's what you're selling.

I AM DEAD

I am dead

Not literally

More like the walking dead

A fucking zombie

Right out of a George Romero film

I shuffle slowly around

Feet scraping the carpet

Tile

Concrete

Asphalt

Or whatever surface is beneath me

My eyes fixed

On nothing in particular

Zoned out

Like I was back in

High school English class

My mind blank

Except for the flashes of memories

I wish I could erase

I am dead

And by dead I mean

I have no heartbeat

Not literally

My heart beats

But with no purpose

My brain functions

But with no real thoughts

About anything important

Just darkness

Foggy

Out of focus

Darkness

A hazy

Cloudy nothingness

With flashes of memories

I wish I could erase

But not sure

If I even want to

I am numb

Numb to everything

I don't want to do shit

I don't want to eat

I can't sleep

I don't want to wake up

Or get out of bed

I wish

I could sleep forever

Not die

(Well maybe)

But because I can't remember

Most of my dreams

Which is something that I used to hate

But now would be a godsend

I don't want to work

Clean

Shit

Shower

Or shave

I am broken

Amputated

Arms

Legs

Head

Detached

And there isn't a doctor

Or nurse

Or shrink

Or Priest

That can put me back together

There is no drug

That can repair my shattered soul

No booze

That can conquer my unruly demons

No mumbo jumbo

That can magically cure my knife-piercing ills

I don't know

What the fuck

I'm going to do now

Maybe I will walk the earth

Like Kane from Kung Fu

Maybe I will sell all of my shit

And walk the earth

Going from town to town

Helping people in need

With my soft spoken Kung Fu skills

Except

I don't have any

Fuck

I don't know what

I am going to do

I am lost

And I can't be found

Ever

The future is frightening

Terrifying

Hopeless

Jobless

Loveless

Lonely

Painful

And every other adjective

You can think of

To describe the horrors of life

I used to think

That life was meaningless

And now I know that it is

I died at the age of thirty four

And now I am the walking dead

A fucking zombie

Slowly shuffling around

In a mindless state
Of pain and suffering
Without direction
Without purpose
Without love.

A SARCASTIC POEM

Life is great

Every morning

I awake

To the sounds

Of birds chirping

Their melodic

Sounds of glee

I smile

As the morning sun

Shines on my

Blemish free

Wrinkle free

Skin

I look

In the mirror

And admire

The perfection

That is my body

I feel

The warm

Shower water

Envelope me

Like an unbelievably

Soft blanket

Not too hot

Not too cold

But just right

I smell

The awesomeness

That is bacon

Sizzling

And dancing

In a chemical free

Non-stick

Frying pan

I taste

The organic

Free-trade

South America

Gourmet coffee

I ground myself

As it slides

Past my tongue

Down my esophagus

Happily filling

My waiting

Stomach

I drive

On an empty freeway

To my amazing

Job

And work

Eight blissful hours

With a huge smile

On my face

Wanting

Wishing

I could work

A couple more

I arrive

Home

My wife

My kids

My pets

Welcome me

With hugs

And kisses

And smiles

And stories

Of their glorious day

Dinner

Is on the table

Three courses

Salad

Steak

And

A warm slice

Of pecan pie

The kids

Go to sleep

Without a fuss

The wife and I

Make love

Like it was

Our first time

We fall asleep

In each other's

Arms

I dream

Not of what I want

But of what I have

And I awake

The next day

Which will be

The best day

Of my life

Is this a sarcastic poem?

Or is the title?

ALLEN GINSBERG

Allen Ginsberg
Is in my heart
He is in my mind
Controlling me
He is in my thoughts
Poisoning me
He is in my soul
Writing these words.

I USED TO CARE

I used to care

About the world's

problems

Politics

Human rights

The environment

Saving the world

One cause at a time

One protest at a time

One letter at a time

To my representatives

Who didn't even give

Two fucks

About what I had to say

They just sat there

Debating

Deliberating

Procrastinating

Masturbating

Doing nothing

As my neighborhood

My city

My state

My country

My planet

Continues to crumble

And slowly disappear

God's gift

Wasting away

As he or she or it or whatever

Shakes his or her or its

Head in utter disappointment

But the politicians

Have not failed us

The corporations

Have not failed us

The world

Has not failed us

God

Has not failed us

We have failed

Ourselves

We have failed

Society

We have failed

Our environment

We have failed

The planet

We have failed

God

The question now is

How are we going to

Fix it

How are we going to

Make it right

Yeah I said

I used to care

But don't believe

Everything you hear.

MY LIFE

My life
Is spiraling
Out of control
The lunacy
Is taking over
The Zen
The insane thoughts
Are winning
The battle
Over the thoughts
Of peace
And love

What is my purpose?
What is our purpose?
What is the meaning
Of all this?
Why am I here?
Why are we here?
It is to work?
Is it to be a cog

In the machine

That is our society?

I am I just a nut?

Or a bolt?

An insignificant

Piece of shit?

We live eighty years

To do what?

To progress our world?

For what reason?

What is the goal?

What is the endgame?

It has to be something else

There has to be more to it

Than just

This existence

Why Can't I just be

A sheep

Like everyone else?

Why can't I just

Live

Blindly

Like the rest of you?

Why can't I just

Stop

Caring

And just

Live?

My life

Is spiraling

Down the drain

Of madness

Traveling through

The pipes

Of insanity

Headed somewhere

Nowhere

Everywhere

The unknown

And all I have to do

To stop it

Is just turnoff

My mind

But I can't

It's impossible

Inconceivable

I guess

It's just

How it's supposed to be.

THE BEACH

I miss
Your sparkling
Blue attraction
Your symphonic
Meditative sounds
Your hypnotic
Rhythmic motions
Your cool
Invigorating breeze
Your aromatic
Salty smell
Your orgasmic
Sandy feel
Your spiritual
Cosmic energy
Your amazing
Colorful sunsets
Your passionate
Tantric essence
Your therapeutic
Healing power

Your peaceful

Repetitive existence

Your imperfect

Perfection

You were my

First love

And you will be

My last

For when my soul

Leaves this world

My body

Will become

A part of you.

I DREAM OF PLACES

I dream of places
I have never seen
Places that have
Filled the souls of others
But not mine
Places which some say
"What's the big deal?"
"It's only a rock"
"It's only a canyon"
"It's only a tree"
"It's only a building"
"A wall"
"A river"
"A mountain"
"An ocean"
But are those not the things
That make our hearts
Explode
With love
And peace
And enlightenment?

Are those not the things

That make life livable?

Are those not the things

That make us who we are?

Who we were?

Who we want to be?

Is nature

Not art?

Are man-made creations

not on that same level?

I dream of people

I have not yet met

People that have filled

The souls and hearts

Of others

But not mine

People who might not be

That important to some

But mean everything

To others

People who will make me feel

Like the man

I am

The man

I want to be

And will be

Are these people

Not worth my time

My ear

My company

My understanding

My friendship

My love

Who is to say

who is worth it?

Who is deserving

Of our belief

That they must

Earn something

That is free?

I do not dream of things

I have not had

Things others feel they need

To fill their souls

Things are just that

Things

Things that falsely fill

Our hearts

And make them

Explode

With the illusion

Of happiness

Someone once said

"The things you own, will end up owning you"

Ain't that the truth?

The truth continues

We crave

What they want us to crave

We eat

What they want us to eat

We dress

How they want us to dress

We drive

What they want us to drive

We watch

What they want us to watch

We read

What they want us to read

We love

Who they want us to love

These things

Do not make us who we are

Yet we let them

These things

Are murdering

Our souls

Our minds

Our hearts

Our entire existence

I dream of

Simplicity

I dream of

Peace

I dream of

Happiness

I dream of

Love

That is all.

I'M TIRED

I'm Tired

Physically

Mentally

Emotionally

Tired of

The work

I have grown

To despise

Tired of

Kids

Not giving two shits

About what I have to say

Tired of

Waking up tired

Every fucking day

Pretending

To be someone

I'm not

But realizing

That I'm not pretending

Tired of

The game

That fake plastic game

Of conversation

Of wondering

Whether or not

Someone thinks

I am worthy

Of their company

Of their time

Tired of

Good days

And bad days

Everyday

Should be the best day

Of your life

Tired of

Waiting

For my mind

To erase

To change

To evolve

To figure shit out

Tired of

Fighting it

But afraid of

What would happen

If I let it

Do what it wants

Tired of caring

Tired of feeling

Tired of hating

Tired of loving

Tired of life.

AND I WAIT

When we met

A spark

Ignited in my heart

And you fanned

The flames

Unintentionally

We grew

Apart

And that fire hid

In the recesses

Of my heart

As time rolled on

Other lovers

Kept me distracted

Determined to destroy

My love for you

But it was too strong

And it was there

Hiding

Waiting

Hoping

Praying

That one day it could

Grow

And win the battle

It had been fighting

For so long

Then came

The reconnection

After many years apart

My love for you took notice

And it was invigorated

As you once again

Fanned its flames

And it grew

And it grew

And it grew

But you were

Taken

So I tried

To hose it down

Like a firefighter

Battling nature's wrath

But it was

Too insane

Like a wildfire

Burning out of control

Now here I am

My heart Ablaze

Engulfed

With my love for you

And you are there

And i wait

And even though

I Know it's too late

I wait

I wait

I wait

And even though

I know our fate

I wait

I wait

I wait.

I AM NOT MAD

I am not mad
But bat shit crazy
Lightning tongue
Fire in my eyes
Lust in my heart
A devilish smirk
Masking thoughts of
Unspeakable pain
And pleasures
And nothing
And everything
Human

I am not mad
But sanely insane
Blurting out
Random thoughts
Barking
Like a wild dog
Dancing
Arms flailing

Under the black lights
In your living room
Teeth grinding
Eyes wide in madness
But I am not mad
Just human.

THE LITTLE COMMIE CAPITALISTS

The little commie capitalists

Walking the sidewalks

In their outrageous outfits

Flying down the sidewalks

On their shitty scooters

Mopeds

And bikes

Loaded

With people

With garbage

With whatever

Driving the streets

Like madmen

Running people down

Without care

The streets are for cars

You fools!

Packing the metro trains

And buses

Like an overloaded

Washing machine

Pushing

Cramming

Squeezing

Hoping

The door will close

Staring

Staring

Staring

At me

Like I'm the Elephant Man

Yes

I'm tall

Yes

I have hair on my face

Yes

I have tattoos on my arms

Yes

I look different

Strange even

But the novelty

Is wearing thin

On my patience

Stop looking at me!

Stop talking to me

Like I know

What you're saying

Stop trying to run me over

Stop with the fucking horn honking

I'm going to kill someone

Soon.

MICHAEL ROSS

Michael Ross

You son-of-a-bitch

Always there

To wake me up

Like an angry parent

On a school day

To slap me in the face

Like a pissed off

Women

After you tell her

You don't love her

Anymore

To shake the cobwebs

From my black widow

Infested mind

To bring me back

From the dead

Your words

Like defibrillator paddles

Shocking my heart

Back to life

One

Two

Three

Clear!

You bastard

You are my rock

You are my anchor

Keeping me grounded

Keeping me at bay

And you try

And you try

And you try

And I love you

For it

But you hate

My thoughts

My decisions

My philosophy

My poetry

and my

Striking good looks

But I still

Love you

Not like a brother

But like you are

A part of me

And know that

I wrote this poem

Because

One,

I want future generations

To know how much

You mean to me

And two,

Because

I'm a son-of-a-bitch too.

I AM MORE

I am more

Than these fucking tattoos

Than this grizzly red beard

Than these stupid goddamn dimples

Than these clouded, foggy blue eyes

Behind these black rimmed Raybans

I am more

Than these wasted college degrees

Than these revolutionary thoughts

Than these unread self-published books

Than these spontaneous, wannabe poems

That I write because I have to

I am more

Than these made in Asia, sweatshop clothes

Than this waste of my time shit job

Than this bleeding, crippled heart

Than this tortured, battered soul

That searches for answers it will never find

I am more...or maybe I'm not.

SUDDENLY LIFE SEEMED SHORT

Suddenly life seemed short

Twisting metal

Amplified chaos

Red and black fluids

Moving slowly

Over areas of flesh and asphalt

Suddenly life seemed short

Chaos fades

Light engulfs

Blinding

Burning the gateway

To my soul

And then darkness

Eternal darkness

Suddenly life seemed short

Darkness ends

Birds sing

Trees sway

Leaves dance

Nature's symphony

Kissing my ears

Suddenly life seemed short

Chaos returns

Red and blue lights

Flashing

Smells of gas

And oil

Can you hear me?

Are you okay?

Suddenly life seemed…

SHE WILL BE THE DEATH OF US

She will be

The death of us

This I promise you

She makes men

Famous

And others

Limbless

She creates

Power

And destroys

Innocence

She makes

Few rich

And many

Suffer

She kills

And rapes

And maims

Too many

To count

She is the terrible beast

That rots our world

A disease

Slowly killing

What we have created

She will be

The death of us.

FEAR

Fear

Fear

And more Fear

Is all I see and hear

On that zombie box

We worship more than God

Tonight at ten the top story is…

Fear

Watch out

For those bullets

Raining down

From the sky

One just might

Come through your roof

And into your head

Those crazy

Gang bangers

Celebrating the New Year

A family of four

Was killed

In a head on accident

By a man

With marijuana in his system

But we won't tell you

That Marijuana

Stays in your system

For thirty days

And the last time he smoked

Was two weeks ago

An apartment building

Caught fire

Killing seven people

Three of those

Children

You better buy a sprinkler system for your home

Here is a conveniently placed ad

From a sprinkler system company

Buy or Die

Watch out for those

Diet pills

They just might kill you

Watch out for those

Mad cow fast food burgers

They just might kill you

Put a harness on your child

So no one can abduct and kill them

Africanized killer bees are coming

To kill you

Minorities are slowly invading

Your gated communities

The suburbs are no longer safe

Close the borders

The illegal Mexicans

Are taking jobs away

From legal Mexicans

But wait

Who will mow our lawns?

and pick our fruits and veggies?

Watch out for those crazy terrorists

What level are we at today?

Level orange?

Holy shit

Don't fly

Stay inside

Duct tape the windows

With plastic

To keep the chemical weapons

From ruining the meatloaf

Please Mr. President

Bomb Afghanistan

Bomb Iraq

Bomb every aspirin factory

In the world

They are creating chemical weapons in there

Bomb France and Germany

They are against us

Because if you're not with us

You must be against us

Bomb the Inner cities

They are breeding grounds for terrorists

While you're at it

Bomb the media

They are spreading

Fear and lies

And also

While you're at it

Come and get me

This poem must be

A violation of the Patriot Act.

I HAVE A DREAM

I have a dream
That one day
Dr. King's dreams
Will become reality.

YESTERDAY I SAW A MAN DIE

Yesterday

I saw a man die

Lifelong dreams

Shattered

Into a billion

Miserable pieces

Decades of

Blood

Sweat

And tears

For nothing

Time wasted

Wasted

Wasted away

Tomorrow

I will see another die.

SO I LIKE TO DRINK

So I like to drink

A few beers

Now and then

So I like to drink

A shot or two

Again and again

So I like to drink

And drink

And drink

But I'm not

An alcoholic

No matter

What you think.

AMERICA THE BEAUTIFUL?

Red
Is for the blood
Of the innocent
Victims
Of imperialism

White
Is for the leaders
Of the US government
And corporations
That exploit
People
All over the world

Blue
Is for the feelings
Of the people
Under the wingtip
Of oppression

America the beautiful?

I CANNOT STOP THE SCREAMS

I cannot stop

The screams

In my head

Bouncing

Off the inside

Of my skull

Why do they

Torment me?

Why do they

Drive me

To the brink

Of insanity?

I need peace

I need Buddha

I need to stop

The screams

But I can't

They are me.

A2Z

Apricots

Bending

Cellophane

Disasters

Evaporating

Fantasies

Gangrene

Hostilities

Igneous

Jargon

Killing

Liasons

Morphing

Narcoleptic

Ocean

Papayas

Queer

Relics

Suffocating

Tangerines

Unicorn

Venom

Wilting

Xylophones

Yes

Zoe.

WARM SUNLIGHT ON MY FACE

Warm sunlight

On my face

Is better than

The thoughts of the day

Napping on the grass

Under a tree

Is better than

Dealing with me

But sometimes

Burning my flesh

With a lighter

Is better than

Becoming a liar

And sometimes

Poisoning my brain

Is better than

Continually going

Insane.

I AM THE NEW REVOLUTION

I am the new revolution

The extreme

The radical

I am the new generation

The thinking

The tyrannical

I am the new revolution

Of thought

Of societies

I am the new generation

Of visionaries

Of philosophies

I am not

The past

I am not

The future

I am

The now.

I OWE YOU NOTHING

I owe you

Nothing

You owe me

Nothing

I owe them

Nothing

You owe them

Nothing

We owe them

Nothing

They owe us

Everything.

YEAH YEAH WHATEVER

Yeah

Yeah

Whatever

I'm tired

Leave me alone

I don't have

All the answers

No one does

Start thinking

For yourself

I'm tired

Of doing it

For you

It's time

Time for you

To feel

What it's like.

TWO MILLION LOST SOULS

Two million

Lost souls

Rotting away

Like forgotten meat

Tucked away

In the back

Of the fridge

Spoiling

Molding

Slowly dying

Waiting

To be thrown away

With the rest

Of the garbage

What did you do

To deserve this?

What was that?

Who are they

To judge you?

Who are they

to treat you like this?

You need

To be cleansed

You need

To get it together

You need

To be given

A second chance

We all deserve

A second chance.

HOW CAN WE LET THEM

How do you tell

A man

With no limbs

War is justifiable?

How do you tell

A mother

Her only son

Was killed

For no reason?

How do you tell

A wife

Whose husband

Was shot

In the head

War is understandable?

How do you tell

A child

That her daddy

Died

For money

And Power?

How can we let

Them

Continue to

Maim

Torture

And Kill

Our sons

Husbands

And fathers?

PEOPLE NEED TO TAKE A CHANCE

People need to

Take a chance

On what?

Everything

All things

This and that

Whatever

Listen to the voices

In your head

That scream

JUMP

Not to your death

But to your new beginning

Your second birth

Get undressed

Cleanse yourself

Of the memories

That need not be

And watch them spiral

Down the drain

Like a cyclone

Of things forgotten
This is your last chance.

WHY?

Why?

Is the question

We should be asking

But we continue

To ignore it

What?

Is the question of the day

What's for dinner?

What's on TV?

What is the meaning

Of life?

I don't know

Go ask someone

who cares

Why do we not ask

Why?

Why do we

Live in fear?

Why do I

Continue

To live this way?

It would be so much easier

To ask

What?

But why?

CANS OF VEGETABLES

Since when

Are human beings

Cans of vegetables

Sitting

Side by side

On a supermarket shelf

Do I have a sign

around my neck

that says

Genius?

Loser?

Outcast?

Dreamer?

Do you have a sign

Around your neck?

Are you a book

Without a table of contents?

I am not

who you want me to be

I am not

who I want to be

I am just me.

A CIVIL WAR HAIKU

Warm northern love twists
With cold southern hate and fear
A perfect storm brews.

THE FUTURE

The future

Is bleak

From my

Perspective

From my

Viewpoint

From my

Detective

Abilities

That I have grown

To recognize

So don't

Patronize me

Or anybody

It's time

To fuck

Everybody

It's time

To fuck

The fuckers

Who are fucking

Our fucking

Existence

Into fucking Oblivion

Fuck it.

POETIC NONSENSE

This poem

Makes no sense

It is not supposed to

I wrote it

To make you

Think

About What?

That is your journey

I'm only a guide

A fucked up guide

But a guide

In the sense of an instigator

Blood is life

And death

Minds grow

But with unimportant

Garbage

Who said

"the best is yet to come?"

An idiot!

The rich

Can only change

The world

Too bad

They don't care

About anyone

But themselves

The world

Is dying

The idea

Is dying

The past

Is dead

Because nobody cares about it

Screw all of you

You're part of the problem

And you are the only solution.

I WANT TO SEE THE WORLD

I want to see

The world

Through your sparkling eyes

Taste her

Through your sensitive tongue

Feel the cold rain

Stinging your bronzed skin

Hear the symphony

In your artistic mind

Smell the sweet fragrance

Of your sweet smelling

Existence

I want to see

The world

Through your eyes

Taste the sweetness

Of her soft flesh

Feel the warm sun

On your perfect face

Hear the lullaby

Of newborn laughter

In your proportionate ears

Smell the sweet fragrance

Of ripe delicious peaches

Do you want to see

The world

Through my eyes?

Taste her

Through my wicked tongue?

Feel the pin pricks

Of jolted nonsense?

Hear the screams

Of chaos

That is my existence?

Smell the stench

Of decaying emotions?

I didn't think so.

I USED TO THINK

I used to think

The world was

Round

But it's really

Square

I used to think

That there was

Justice

But life is really

Unfair

I used to think

That people were

Kind

But that is not

The case

I used to think

That roses were

Beautiful

But it was really just

The vase.

WHO IS THAT KNOCKING?

Who is that knocking

On my door?

Or should I say

What?

I did not call anyone

I did not tell anyone

To come over

Who is that knocking

on my door?

Is it for me?

Or are they looking

For someone else?

Go away!

Leave me alone!

There is no one here

There is no one here

Who is that knocking

On my door?

What do they want?

Why are they here?

What are they going to do to me?

Who are you?

Who are you?

There is no one here!

Who is that knocking

On my door?

Should I open it?

Should I see who it is?

What should I do?

What should I do?

I am losing

My mind

Who is that knocking

on my door?

What am I afraid of?

Who am I afraid of?

I used to be

Fearless

I used to be

Afraid

Of nothing

Screw it

I will just open it

And end all this

Madness

I will

Here I go

And to no surprise

Death had come

To take me away.

THE GOOD TIMES

The good times

Are catching up

As the raindrops

Approach

Too fast

For me to bear though

Don't really want to go

Things are back and forth

Up and down

Like a fucking out of control

Rollercoaster

Jumping the track

Into an unknown abyss

Of what's to come

Sometimes

I say I can't

Sometimes

I say I have to

Sometimes

I punch the wall

Or the door

Or the fridge

Sometimes

I smoke a cigarette

Sometimes

I cry

Sometimes

All of the above.

WHAT THE FUCK?

What the fuck?

It didn't feel like

Forty two

Red and blue lights

Flashing

From a fancy motorcycle

Shit

What do I do with this

Cigarette?

Damn

I wanted to drink that

Can I see your driver's license?

Vehicle registration?

And proof of insurance?

Do you know

what the speed limit is?

(Lying) no

I usually don't go this way

Is it thirty?

It's twenty five

Twenty five?

Are you kidding me? (thinking, not saying)

Do you know

How fast you were going?

Too fast

That's why you stopped me (thinking not saying)

(Lying) thirty nine or forty?

I clocked your speed at

Forty two

Damn

Seventeen over

No way

I'm getting out of this one

Sir

I had to write you a ticket

You HAD to write me a ticket

Or make your quota (thinking, not saying)

Have a good day

And make sure

You wear your seatbelt

Damn

Guess he let me off the hook

On that one

240 bucks

For a speeding ticket?

What the fuck?

I guess I'm headed

To traffic school

185 bucks

For traffic school?

What the fuck?

Four hours

At the Residence Inn

Meeting room

Four hours

Of learning shit

I already know

Four hours

Of jail time

For speeding

What a waste

Of my fucking time

And 185 bucks

What the Fuck?

15 DAYS IN TENT CITY (THE POEM)

I arrived at Lower Buckeye Jail

On a Saturday

Grabbed my garbage bag

Two officers came out and told us

To get into two lines

Looked over my paperwork

Given a medical form

Take off your shoes

And put our hands on the fence

Walked into the building

I was there for twelve hours

I was determined not to eat

Mug shots taken

Holding cell

Fingerprints

Smaller cell

Handcuffed two of us together

Shackled the two of us together

This is when I really felt life a prisoner

Walked to a van that was waiting outside

Another small cell

Handcuffed two of us together

New home for fifteen days

Searched us

Let us inside

Where we waited

To get our ID cards

And our tent/bunk numbers

Given two pink blankets and a pink towel

Tent 58, bunk 19

Top bunk

Three inch pad for a mattress

Back hurts just thinking about it

Amazing how humans think and act

Hopped into my bunk

Read a little

Went to sleep

It was a long day

Spent most of the day

In my bunk

Reading

And taking naps

Vending machine snacks

Used the restroom

I can still smell

That horrible stench

Got some water

Clean shaven

Box filled

With single blade disposable razors

Cheap bars of soap

Cut myself once

Huge fan in tent

Helped a little with the heat

But still sweated a ton

Hard to sleep

Loud speaker calling

Complaining

Every hour

Lock down

Head count

Every three hours

Up at 4:30am

5:45am everyone over to the gate

Twelve hours out

Drove home

Showered

Went to work

Went home

Watched the news

And then Jeopardy

Shaved

Changed

Headed back at 5:00pm

Waiting outside the gate

Belts off

Shoes off

Socks off

And everything out of your pockets

Put your hands on the fence

And spread our legs

Pat down

Check each shoe

Head in

Vending machines

Red licorice

My little night time snack

To my bunk

Laid down

Read

Tried to sleep

New book

Philosophy

Guys spit game

To females as we wait

To check in

Guess it's easier

Since we're in the same boat

But who cares

I'm not here to meet chicks

Searched by cute female guard

Bonus

Later see the females

When they get to use our vending machines

Bunk-mate always lifts the side of our tent

So we can see them walk to the door

This is our entertainment

My bunk-mate is a beauty critic

"No, no, no, yes, no, yes, no, etc…

"There's one for you"

"Big girls need love too"

Shit is too funny

Back in my bunk

Read a little

Try to sleep

Caught a kid trying to smuggle a cigarette

In his ass crack

Placed in handcuffs

Sat him to the side

Now the rest of us got the super pat down

Swiped my ass crack

And each side of my junk

Like he was using his ATM card

To buy some groceries

Got in

Red licorice

Shot the shit

Went to my bunk

Read for a little bit

Ate my red licorice

Tried to get some sleep

Not every bunk was filled

Five hundred inmates

Each inmate paying eighty dollars a day

"The man" is bringing in forty grand a day

Over fourteen million clams a year

Orange sleep drink

Bought two

Drank one on the drive

Then one while I waited to enter

Slept most of the weekend

New book

On the Road

Patted-down

Entered the yard

Snacks for the weekend

Noise

Coming from the loud speaker

Pigeons

People getting up

Laid in bed

In and out of sleep

Went out into the yard

Bullshitted with some guys

New group of fresh meat

We counted forty five

Man people need to stop drinking and driving

A young kid walked

Holding his mattress

Somebody fell for the old

Go get your mattress inspected by an officer gag

We laughed

As he walked up to the officer

Who pointed past our tent

Shook his head

And flipped those guys off

We were rolling

Classic jailhouse comedy

"They got you huh"

"Yeah"

Went into the yard

Bullshitted

Not allowed to smoke

But some did anyway

People throw stuff over the fence

In the middle of the night

Crazy bastards

Cigarettes

Two bucks a piece

Basic economics

Supply and demand

Two bucks for something

That cost only about forty cents on the outside

Sundays the price jumped

To three bucks a smoke

These guys know economics

The Sheriff also knows a little about economics

A buck twenty five

For a Snickers

Woke up

My first jail meal

Chow as it is called

A clear bag containing

Two hoagie style pieces of bread

Two slices of bologna

An orange

An oatmeal cookie/pie thing

The kind with the white cream in the middle

And two small cartons of milk

Walked over to my bunk

Looked over my spread

Didn't want my milk

Gave it to my bunk-mate

I wanted some peanut butter

My bunk-mate gave me some

He had nine servings in hiding

Ate the orange like a caveman

Ate the oatmeal cookie/pie thing

No way was I eating the bologna

Jumped up on my bunk

And read from On the Road

Spent most of the day

In my bunk

Sleeping

And reading

Lock-down

Head count

Every three hours

In our bunks

ID's out

Everyone has their ID affixed to their bunk

With a rubber band

Wind was crazy

Felt like a tornado was right on top of us

Tent was flapping like mad

And was super close to slapping me

In the face

Waiting to be searched

Girl in the waiting area

Acting weird

Picked up a rubber glove

Reached into her pocket

Put something in the glove

Squatted behind two trashcans

And stuck the glove you know where

I couldn't believe what I was seeing

Entered the yard

Went to my tent

Bullshitted

Female commissary entertainment

Read

Tried to get some sleep

Rained like crazy

Dark clouds coming

Good old fashioned Arizona monsoon

Rain began to seep through our tent

Right above my bunk

Water began to slowly drip on me

Took my two pink towels

And wrapped them around the steel frame

Above my bunk

Night and morning

Cold

Rough night of sleep

Guy screaming and yelling

No idea what was going on

Found out later

Black male

Mid-twenties

Smoked some spice

Synthetic marijuana

Wouldn't wake up

They slapped him in the face

He flipped out

Started screaming and yelling

Ran to the jail office

Taken away in an ambulance

Jailhouse chili burritos

Interesting how people

Who have been in the system

Discover creative ways

To not only eat

But do other things as well

Horseshoes

Bottles half full of rocks

Throwing them into a garbage can

Back and forth

Mini-me

Younger version of me

Twenty one

Majoring in civil engineering

Only has four classes left

Cool kid

Bullshitted

Finished On the Road

Left it for the "library"

Woke up

To the sound of the loud speaker

Someone shit in the showers

Unbelievable

Who does that

Probably this new weird guy

That looked like he was homeless or something

He ate three trays of that slop

No one does that

Learned how to play spades

And won my first and only game

Day was long

Hot

Boring

Slept a little

Bullshitted a little

Read

And waited

And waited

And waited

10:45pm

The call on the loud speaker came

I grabbed my things

Exited the yard

Two by two

Walked to the main office

Placed in a holding cell about twelve by twelve

Forty of us

Waited thirty minutes

Handcuffed us to another guy

Cuffed to mini-me

Loaded on a bus

Further tortured us

By blaring country music

On the ride over

Officer that loaded us up

A tall hunchback motherfucker

Looked like the mutant guy from The Devil's

Rejects

We entered a room

Removed our handcuffs

Threw them in a crate

Must be a heavy son-of-a-bitch

They have to drag it out

If that mutant officer drags it out

It would be just like the opening scene of The

Devil's Rejects

Where the mutant guy

Is dragging a naked dead woman

By the hair

Sure enough he dragged it out

I started laughing

It was classic

Stuffed into an eight by fifteen cell

Standing room only

Four cells occupied

Three with us guys

And one with some ladies

Fingerprinted us

In another cell

Immigration and Customs Enforcement

Ice Ice Baby

Wanted to talk to me

They thought I was Canadian

Really

"Where were you born"

"California"

"What are the first three digits of your social

security number"

"557"

"How long have you been in Arizona"

"Since 2003"

"Okay"

Back to the cell

Waited longer

Names were called

Lined up in front of a big, long desk

An officer called us up

One at a time

I was called second

Asked me questions from my file

To make sure it was me being released

Full name

What I was charged with

What court I was charged in

Address

Year of birth, etc

We entered a little room

Door closed behind us

Another door buzzed

Opened it

We were outside

Exited another door

Freedom

A great feeling

Fifteen days in Lower Buckeye Jail

Interesting experience

That I will never experience again.

I love and miss you dad

(T.A. Maxwell Sr. 1954-2012)

Also by T.A. Maxwell

The Zen Lunatics
Broken Like Vinyl
On the Road to Big Blackfoot
Into The Ocean
Sexy, Smart, Crazy Beautiful

www.ingramcontent.com/pod-product-compliance
Lightning Source LLC
Chambersburg PA
CBHW031557040426
42452CB00006B/334